GRANDPARENTS

Other books by Charlie W. Shedd

TALK TO ME!
LETTERS TO KAREN
LETTERS TO PHILIP
THE FAT IS IN YOUR HEAD

Also

SMART DADS I KNOW
GETTING THROUGH TO THE WONDERFUL YOU
THE EXCITING CHURCH WHERE PEOPLE REALLY PRAY
THE EXCITING CHURCH WHERE THEY REALLY USE THE BIBLE
THE EXCITING CHURCH WHERE THEY GIVE THEIR MONEY AWAY
IS YOUR FAMILY TURNED ON?
PROMISES TO PETER (YOU CAN BE A GREAT PARENT)
THE STORK IS DEAD
THE PASTORAL MINISTRY OF CHURCH OFFICERS
HOW TO DEVELOP A PRAYING CHURCH
TIME FOR ALL THINGS
HOW TO DEVELOP A TITHING CHURCH

CHARLIE W. SHEDD

GRANDPARENTS

Then God created grandparents
and it was very good

Doubleday & Company, Inc.
Garden City, New York

ISBN: 0-385-11067-7
Library of Congress Catalog Card Number 75-42892
15   14   13   12   11

Photos courtesy of John Hill except those by Dorothy Hill on pages 20, 108, 115, and 122, and by Sven Martson on pages 16, 21, 23, 28, 37, 40, 44, 52, 70, 71, 80, 95, 96, 97, 102, 116, 121, 130, and 135.

To Van and Treva Jane
very special friends
very special grandparents

Preface

You can be a fun grandparent. I know some secrets and the reason I know them is that many people have told me their secrets. So I know you can be the kind we would all like to be—interesting, helpful, nice to remember.

Authors have a tremendous reservoir of "what for" and "how to." I do. Young, old, and in-between write me. They've been reading my newspaper column, "Strictly for Dads." Or they are listeners to my ninety-second radio spot, "Parent Talk." They tell me everything from trivia to intimate details.

Do you suppose I'm prejudiced? I think my readers are the most beautiful people in the world. I know they're out there. I ask one question and here comes a blizzard of response. Correspondence from everywhere about everything. They tell me, "I like you," "I don't like you," and "Here's what I think."

Some subjects are a sure thing, and one of these is grandparents. Seems the whole world enjoys talking about grandparents. Children like to talk about grandparents. Grownups too. The busy businessman, his office girl, housewives, college students. Professors. And grandparents? Do they ever like to talk about grandparents!

So I've been asking all these people, "What's a grandparent for?" "What do you remember most about yours?" "What kind of grandparent do you want to be?"

A lot of the things they've told me I want to share with you.

But these are not my premier input. For the past eight years I've been living with a super grandmother. Fortunately for me she never runs out of love. For life. For the world around her. For all kinds of people. And a special kind for her husband. Then in these past eight years I've noticed something new. There is also a special kind of love for grandparenting. So she and I have been discussing this business. Like you, we want to do it right.

You would too if you could see our three little granddaughters. And then there are all those little grandsons and more little girls coming on. For all of these we want to be the best kind of grandparents.

We know our grandchildren *are* the best. But we also know you think yours are. So let's settle for the fact that yours are the best for you and ours are the best for us. (Now that's a very fair offer, isn't it, since we know ours *really* are superior?)

Yet no matter who's doing the boasting, we can surely agree on one thing. Somebody these days better be caring, loving, guiding. And in a world where foundations are being shaken, this is great to know—some solid builders are still at work. Who are the solid builders? I think some of the best are grandpas and grandmas.

Contents

Grandparents are for holding hands and smiling at each other . . . My grandmother makes me think that God is her best friend . . . Sometimes when it is quiet, they will even talk to you about heaven.

GRANDPARENTS

I

What are grandparents for?

Grandparents are for wondering with you

"Grandma, why isn't milk green?"

Reasonable question under the circumstances.

We were visiting my sister in Wisconsin. She and her husband had a big dairy herd. This was the first of many visits and were they ever a sight about sundown in the pasture. Black and white Holstein. Deep green grass. Lush. Then we watched the milking process done by machine. Next we went to their little creamery. Here the fascinating separator did its thing. Out of this spout, milk. Out of that, cream.

Grandma was with us. Since she was one of our favorite people, she often went where we went.

Suddenly at dinner, a question. Holding his big glass of pure white milk, he turned and said, "Grandma, why isn't milk green?"

So why isn't it?

Of course, he would ask grandma. Grandparents are for wondering. For wondering with, wondering about, just wondering.

A grandparent is for awe. For speculating on things nobody ever thought before. Mothers and dads can't think about things like this. They don't have time.

We think it was Paul Jim who asked it. He's our middle son and for some reason cows really turned him on. Often.

One of our favorite things was to go riding in the country. The whole family. Great time to visit. Plan. Make important decisions. But when Paul Jim was not quite two, we had a problem. We couldn't get past a cow without a

15

barrage of "Moo! moo! moo!" His sister counted nineteen times per cow. So with a sizable herd, this stuff got heavy. But wasn't it also a little bit wise?

Sad how we become calloused to life's wonders. Cows really *are* special. They have so much to give. Milk and strong bones. Meat and the smell of rib roast. Hide and shoes on our feet. Horns, hoofs, and the glue we used last week. Let the case rest. A bovine is a mighty creature.

> And except we become as little children,
> we cannot enter the kingdom of heaven.

DADDY'S MUCH TOO BUSY

Small boy in Sunday School: Today's theme was heaven and he was sure he wanted to go. He would also want his mother there. In fact, he was so

enthused, he'd even take his sister. But his daddy? Not much chance there. Probably his daddy couldn't get away from the office.

Most fathers are busy gunning for another promotion. And why not? It takes some doing to bring home those big beautiful dollars. Somebody has to keep food on the table, buy shoes, clothes, pay doctor bills.

And mother? She cooks, cleans, does so many things at the church. On Tuesday she's a pink lady at the hospital. Wednesday she golfs. She also plays bridge, belongs to the prayer group, takes Fido to the vet. Friday, she drives the car pool.

So what's a grandparent for? Could it be the Lord made grandparents for total focus?

"Come back, come back, look at the seeds."

We were crossing the street at the feed store. The light turned green. I started across when I heard that excited little voice calling, "Come back, come back, look at the seeds."

So I turned and there was one of my favorite people on hands and knees. She was studying something on the walk, chanting in the beautiful litany of a four-year-old, "I wonder what they grow?"

So down I went to join the worship, and we mused together. "Would they grow a pumpkin? Watermelon? bush, flower, tree?"

To all, same answer: "We don't know."

Then the benediction:

> "Thank you, grandpa, for looking
> at the seeds with me."

Children do have the capacity to be completely absorbed in multitudinous things. That pretty rock, this bug, the magnetic catch on our cupboard door, how a cat stretches, pictures on the dog food can.

Now into this awesome reverie comes the rasping sound—"Dinner is ready." "Wash your hands." "Empty the trash." "Time for bed."

So the little scientist narrows his scope, turns down his imagination, sets aside his curiosity. Once more, some harassed and harried adult snatches him back to the big people's world. Turn off your imagination. Hurry!

Still, "Why isn't milk green, grandma?"

"Who has time to wonder with me?"

Grandpa. Grandma.

Grandparents are for listening

Brinton is a busy oil company executive. He lives in New York City which is a hurry-up town. Plus he has an important job. Decisions, decisions, and mostly about people. So in his particular capacity, he must try hard to understand the other fellow's point of view.

Brinton is a grandfather now. Since he is one of the best friends I ever had, he would tell me things he might not tell other people. But I wanted to pass on one of his thoughts, so I wrote him. "Could I quote this section from your letter? I think it might help all of us grandfathers."

Green light.

"Our three granddaughters were coming for their summer visit. And for me that was too soon after Christmas. All their noise and activities were a far piece from our normal quiet. By the time they left on New Year's Day, Pat had to peel me off the wall. She said I was making noises like, 'Next time we'll move to a motel and turn the house over to them.' That was one of my printable quotes.

"Well, Pat sat me down and gave me a talking to. 'You've got to come down off your high and mighty. Tune out the long distance calls, the contracts, board meetings. Set your receiver for some little people talk. What do their noises mean? Listen. Really listen. Listen to what they're thinking, what they're saying, what they're feeling. You'll be surprised what you can learn. Besides it could be fun.'

"I promised I'd give it a try. So they came. Two, five, six-and-a-half. Would you believe I had a marvelous two weeks with those kids. Funny thing, their high-pitched screams weren't all that awful. Seems like tuning in to them, I tuned out some of the stuff in my own head which must have been turning the volume up.

"It was a great summer vacation. I had more fun than I'd ever had, and they did too. In fact, just last night we were talking long distance. They said they could hardly wait till this Christmas when they could see grandpa and grandma again. Know something? I'm looking forward to it too."

Somewhere along the line certain of us caught a common disease—selfishness. It's one of those sinister hangers-on which never seems to go away. We try. We make it a while. Then here it comes again making us less than we'd like to be.

Maybe this is one of those toughies Jesus had in mind when He said, "This kind goeth not out but by prayer."

> Lord, give me the strength to break old habits.
> I am so prone to think of me first,
>   me second, me third.
> Then if there's anything left,
> I'll take that too.
> School me for the art of tuning in to others,
>   listening, caring.

QUESTION: As I grow older, am I becoming less selfish?
More selfish?

THANKS FOR YOUR WONDERFUL ADVICE

He was a young man and I was a young minister in Nebraska. He came to my study that day with a problem. For two hours he poured out his story.

During the course of that two hours, all I remember saying was, "yes," "no," "I understand." "go on." And "no," "yes" some more.

When he had finished, he rose with an expression of tremendous relief. Then he sighed a deep sigh, reached across the desk, seized my hand and said, "I will never be able to thank you, Reverend, for your wonderful advice."

With that, he was gone.

In talking his problem out, he had seen the answer clearly. I suppose he thinks to this day that he had met a brilliant counselor.

So hard for me to understand . . .

> People of every age are
> helped more by what *they*
> say than by what I say.

And that may be especially important for me to remember as a grandparent.

Grandparents are for saying "no" sometimes

Some interesting observations come from church school classes. This was fifth grade and it was the Sunday for their pastor's visit. Good visit. We had been discussing grandparents. Some thought their grandparents were neat because they weren't always saying "no," "don't," "you can't."

But one astute young man observed, "My grandparents aren't always like that. Sometimes they tell me 'no,' and I think that's O.K."

Right then the bell rang, so we didn't have time for follow-up. It was only one line from a small boy, but I've thought about it often. What did he have in mind? From what I've seen close up, I think it could be this: Children like to know where the fences are! Well-defined limits give them security, and that's an important note for grandparents.

Sometimes our grandchildren don't actually want what they say they want. What they really want right now is the firm voice of authority.

They'll plan. They'll plead. They'll try to maneuver us. But then one day when things get scary, they'll thank us for "no," "don't," "you can't." Which for us may not be easy. Some words come slow when the hair turns gray.

YOU BE IN BY MIDNIGHT

One of my interesting letters in the grandparent category comes from a high school junior.

> Dear Dr. Shedd:
> Can you help me decide something? You remember I told you before how my folks just don't get along. Last year they sent me to stay with my grandparents. Now they want me to come home. Well, I don't mind so much leaving all my friends here, because I have a lot of friends there too.
> Only I'm afraid what would happen again. They fight with each other so much, they never pay attention to my brothers and me. It may sound funny to you, but one of the things I like best here is when my grandfather says, "You be in by midnight." Or my grandmother tells me, "Sally, we can't let you do that so long as we are responsible." It makes me feel like they really care.

Say it again, grandpa. You too, grandma.

Security comes from knowing where the boundaries are. It's a panicky feeling to be too much on your own too soon.

(Time now for a parenthesis. More and more on today's scene we see grandparents raising their grandchildren. Part time, full time, too much of the time, saddled with total responsibility.

(So here's a tip of the hat to these heroes. Bringing up one family ought to be enough. But where it has to be two, may this be their reward—a special assignment in heaven with the single directive: "You check in over here, folks, and spend the first thousand years being silly old grandparents.")

27

We come in many sizes. Tall, short, round, skinny (lucky few). We come in every color, creed, class. Very old, like in the storybooks. And then there are some grandparents so young it's hard to believe. But though we have many differences, most of us coalesce around this strange phenomenon. When we think about our grandchildren, it's nothing but the best for the best.

> He was a regal-looking gentleman. I'd never seen him before. He'd come to my study that day, because his wife had sent him. And I liked his straightforward approach. "I'm having an argument with my son-in-law. My wife thinks he's right. I've been working on trust funds for my grandchildren's education. Spent a lot on spadework. Wouldn't you think anyone would go for a deal like that? Not Tommy. He told me in no uncertain terms he wanted to educate his own children.
>
> "I think he's being silly. So what do you think?"

Sorry, gramps, you knocked on the wrong door. I put in with your wife and your son-in-law.

No grandparent has the right to take away from fathers and mothers the right to do their own parenting.

I've known a few grandmas who left their head behind when they took off for the shopping center. But from what I've seen and experienced firsthand, this is mostly a grandfather ailing.

"You know I couldn't do all these things when my own children were little. I worked hard. Shouldn't I spend my money the way I want?"

Sounds reasonable. We get so much pleasure from giving. It makes us feel good. But what if we hurt our grandchildren while we're doing some good for us? Some necessary lessons only come by toughing it through alone.

Straight from the grandparent front, a story. I've heard it in several versions, but this one I need for my grandfathering.

Ronnie was twelve. Outside his bedroom window he spotted a gray cocoon. Grandpa told him if he watched it closely, that ball of fuzz would break open and out would come a butterfly.

Sure enough, that's exactly how it happened. Only it took so long. Before he knew it, Ronnie was pushing and straining too. Suddenly, he had a bright idea. He would take his knife and cut around the end to set the butterfly free. Beautiful!

Only, you know! Sad! Several times the butterfly tried to take off, but couldn't. So at last it gave up and died. What would you do if you were a little boy with a dead butterfly in your hand and wonder in your eyes? Well, if you had a grandpa in the house like this little boy's grandpa, you'd go to him. And you would learn something important when he said, "Ronnie, the butterfly needed to fight its way out. That's how it gets strength to fly."

Fine lesson for a child, isn't it? And should I be doing a retake on the same lesson for my grandchildren? In any way, am I cutting the cocoon too soon?

Grandparents are for having fun with you

A friend of mine is chaplain to the prisoners in one of our western penitentiaries. He works with drug addicts and pushers serving time. He speaks often to P.T.A.'s, church groups, wherever families gather. And he gives this interesting witness, "Whenever parents ask me, 'How can I keep my children off drugs?' I say, 'Have fun.'"

From what I've seen that is right on target.

Nobody knows all the reasons why some turn to drugs and some don't. But to find out straight from where it's happening, or isn't, my publisher and I conducted a survey. We gave away hundreds of dollars for the best essays on "Why I Don't Use Drugs."* Thousands of entries came from cool young citizens who had thought it through and opted not to go this route.

And here's the good news: Those who said "no" looked back to their homes with happy recall!

F U N, spell it with caps. Spell it "protective therapy." Spell it trips together and sessions around the family table. Spell it good times shared and communication. Spell it many ways, but sometimes, spell it "grandpa," "grandma."

"My grandmother was my very best friend. I
mean my best friend ever. The winter before she
died, she came to live where we did. Only she had
an apartment on the corner. Every night I'd get off

* *Is Your Family Turned On?*, Charlie W. Shedd, Word, Inc., 1971.

The nicest compliment one grandmother ever received: "Grandma, I'll be glad when I'm as old as you are, so I'll have as much fun as you do."

the school bus and stop to see her. She would
always be waiting for me by the window. Then
we ate some cookies, had hot chocolate, lemonade,
played games. We played "kings and queens" and
sometimes animals. She could meow exactly like
a cat, and bark almost like a dog. We also played
movie stars and people from our favorite TV
programs. I could talk about everything around my
grandma and imagine anything. She wouldn't
laugh at me. Grandparents are the most fun,
because they aren't afraid to pretend."

What a gift for a child—the gift of a stage to act out all his fantasies. One place where he can dream on uninhibited. This too grandparents are for.

"Grandmothers will laugh at all your jokes and they even have some of their own. But they will not tell you dumb jokes like lots of grown people tell."

"My grandfather and I have the most fun asking each other riddles. I don't know where he gets the ones he asks me, but they are sure good."

"Grandparents are like this. When you tell them you want to do something, they will say that is what they want to do. They will even say it when they don't exactly mean it. But after they do it with you, they will have fun anyway."

Stan and Esther live by the sea. This year when their granddaughter visited them, she was walking the beach alone. You know what happened. She's sixteen and gorgeous. So the handsome young man from somewhere thought she might be lonely. That very evening they were having this big party and all his friends would be there. Wouldn't she like to go?

When she told him she was visiting her grandparents, spending the evening with them, he asked, "What's the matter with you? Don't you want to have some fun?"

"Oh," she answered, "you should see the fun I have with my grandparents."

Grandparents are for telling you what it used to be like, but not too much

Grandmother, on a winter's day,
Milked the cows and fed them hay,
Slopped the hogs, saddled the mule
And got the children off to school;
Did the washing, mopped the floors,
Washed the windows, and did some chores,
Cooked a dish of home-dried fruit,
Pressed her husband's Sunday suit,
Swept the parlor, made the bed,
Baked a dozen loaves of bread,
Split some firewood, and lugged in
Enough to fill the kitchen bin;
Cleaned the lamps and put in oil,
Stewed some apples she thought would spoil;
Cooked a supper that was delicious
And afterward washed up the dishes;
Fed the cat and sprinkled the clothes,
Mended a basketful of hose;
Then opened the organ and began to play,
"When you come to the end of a perfect day."*

* It's an oldie. I've heard it attributed miscellaneous ways. But whoever the anonymous country poet, thanks!

Nostalgia is big these days. It always has been big with grandpas and grandmas. We love to remember. Back when the children were small . . . the first baby . . . when Philip learned to walk so early, talk so early, brilliant . . . Those first days at school . . . When Karen played pink angel in the Christmas pageant . . . Peter's home run with the bases loaded . . . Paul's straight "A" cards . . . And Timothy's funny, funny readings . . . Remember those rides in the country? . . . The hills? Sheep grazing? That mother pheasant with all her little pheasants? Vacations at the lake . . . How we all get together at Christmas . . . When we moved after a long debate, and everything turned out super.

Remember that tree outside our window? Was it really all that beautiful? Or could it be that we were newly married and everything was beautiful? Then the tree went down one day in a heavy wind. Isn't it nice our own roots have held?

Great how the Lord does our recall. Somehow the negative fades. The good times keep coming on strong, stronger.

These are rough days for some of the elderly. Economy closes in and with it new worries. Shrinking pensions. Friends phasing out.

So where is our happiness?

One answer for sure is memories. Memories of people. "Happening" memories. "Thing" memories.

Be careful, grandma. Watch it, grandpa. You can be a big fat bore. Or a tall skinny one. Or a little bitty puckery prune nobody wants to listen to.

> He was a bore
> Much to my sorrow
> He was here today
> And here tomorrow.

WHAT'S THE DIFFERENCE?

Straight from the youth front comes the message—"All my friends like my grandparents. They tell you these neat things about when they were young, but they don't try to make it sound perfect. They also tell dumb things they did. They are so funny."

That's one important clue for the right kind of historical communication. If we can make them laugh with us, that's good. If we can make them laugh *at* us, they like that too.

"My grandmother lives with us and I get tired listening to her. She's always talking about how it used to be. You would think nothing ever happened worth anything since she was a girl."

CONCLUSION: Young lives facing forward won't mind some facing back. But when we get to "pining," they'll tune us out. Yesterday wasn't a better day for them. They're dreaming of tomorrow.

"Things couldn't have been as bad as they say. Walking twenty miles every day to school in the snow, freezing? You know what they're trying to tell us? How easy we have it today. That's a drag!"

Another tip for our grandparenting: "All the people were heroes back there" simply won't play in young hearts. All the early citizens weren't paragons of virtue. Besides, what if they were?

"Hey, grandpa, come here. Listen. Did you ever hear that tune?"

Did I! That's Wayne King and "The Waltz You Saved for Me." And here's my grandson absolutely ape over the old, old oldies. But isn't it because *he* discovered them? One day he tuned in to the station where they've caught on to an interesting switch. Nostalgia is big with the young set if it's right. But it better be right.

THE GOOD OLD DAYS?

Back to our childhood home. Whatever happened to all those memories? Has that apple tree shrunk or did our imagination make it bigger? The old swimming hole so muddy? No longer pure and crystal? Is my mind playing tricks? Don't I remember clear blue water? And the hill over there! That glorious sweeping slide! Or was it ever so sweeping? Do hills change all that much in forty years or seventy?

Were the good old days not all that good?

"Grandparents are for telling you what it used to be like, but not too much."

CONSERVATIVE-LIBERAL

"Conservative" is a dirty word for the young unless it's handled properly.
Meaning what?
Meaning the right blend of "conservative" and "liberal."
Nothing will turn the young off quite so fast as

>Come weal, come woe
>My status is quo.

Definitions for musing:

A HEALTHY CONSERVATIVE cherishes the good from yesterday. He respects those things his fathers fought for. He cares about bringing along values out of the past. But he is also willing to let go those things which have outlived their usefulness.

The HEALTHY LIBERAL looks to tomorrow with hope. He is grateful for good things previously done, but he doesn't adulate the past. Because this is true, he can move to correct old errors. And he is willing to try new things.

Many of today's young appear to be completely turned off by any idea from yesterday. Some of them really are. Forever.

But countless of these who appear to be turned off aren't really that turned off. They aren't that turned off to democracy. They aren't that turned off to our constitutional heritage. Nor to history. What they are turned off to is any of us who are overly turned on to days gone by.

As I rap with them, I find they are willing to see good in the past, provided. Provided what? Provided I remain flexible enough to believe:

(a) All the good hasn't been done.

(b) They can make a contribution too.

So here is another absolute essential if I am to communicate with my grandchildren. I must have in my head and heart a touch of the poet's philosophy:

> The best verse hasn't been rhymed yet.
> The best world hasn't been planned.

Hell comes in different forms.

And one is what the preacher gets when he relocates a church building. I should know. I presided over such a move in an Oklahoma parish. The dear "old" edifice had been there for as long as natives could remember. Downtown. Too little parking. No room for expansion. Looking for all the world like a cross between some Moslem Mosque and the First National Bank. What kind of architecture this? "Early Oil."

Our committees on "what to do now" had come in with their reports. Someone had given us an eight-acre site, three miles to the east. "Way out in the country," they said. "They" being the mature ladies' class. Grandmothers all.

The committee brought in graphs, charts, projections on population growth. This was the way to go, the only possible direction our town could accommodate new residents.

But "they" just sat there, stone-faced, stolid. Looking for all the world like the figures in Grant Wood's *American Gothic*.

Of course, I took it on the chin. Somebody has to be the whipping boy. Why not the young minister?

Then right in the middle of the heat and frenzy, a letter. It was a brief handwritten note from Ida. Ida was a member of the class, and a leader. Obviously Ida had been biding her time. "Stay with it, preacher," she wrote. "Thought you might like to know our class isn't 100% against you. The longer I live, the clearer I see young folks *are* sometimes right about what's best for the future."

Thank you, Ida.

How many times have I drawn on the thrill of that moment. What seemed too impossible, wasn't. Praise God for one little crack in the status quo.

The grandparent who can achieve a proper blend of conservative and liberal will be more attractive to his grandchildren. He will be more pleasant to have around. And more respected.

Benediction for grandpas and grandmas:

> May you often be right, but not always
> So even when you're old and all-knowing
> May it also occur to you,
>   you might possibly be wrong.

"Lord, for whatever influence I can be today, help me to find the right mix of yesterday and tomorrow."

Grandparents are for saying, "I think you're O.K."

"The thing I like about my grandpa is how he keeps saying, 'I know you can make first chair. When some of those seniors graduate, you'll slip right in there. You can believe your old grandad, Jeannie! I can tell a good fiddle every time.' But here's the funny part. I'm not even playing the violin. I play viola. Only I haven't told him because I still like the way he says it."

"When my father says, 'You are so dumb,' that always makes me feel just terrible. So when I can, I go to see my grandmother and tell her about it. Then she says, 'I think what you did is not so good. But you're O.K.'"

"You asked for stories about grandparents, and I would like to tell you mine. I have three wonderful children and a perfectly marvelous husband. But I wouldn't even be here if it hadn't been for my grandparents. When I was seventeen, I thought I was in love, and you probably know what happened. I got pregnant. My folks were super-religious and you wouldn't be-

lieve the way they took it. They told me I was going to hell, and said all kinds of horrible things. You know, the family image. How could they ever face their friends again? They kept it quiet as long as they could. Then they sent me away. And I gave my baby up for adoption. Even when I came back home, they watched me like a hawk. They kept running me down and acted so hurt. They made me feel like I was the worst person in the world.

"But one day my grandparents sat me down and said, 'You're not really all that terrible. You mustn't be so down on yourself. Some day you'll meet a man, a real man, and he will love you like we do. We think you have grown so much. You're wiser, more beautiful, more ready to love. From now on when you get down on yourself, remember some people are up on you. Like the parents of your baby. You did a great thing for them, didn't you? And we're up on you too.'"

Then she goes on page after page, writing her hymn of praise. A song of gratitude for two people in her life with X-ray vision. This too is a part of good grandparenting—to see merit through the negative.

II
What my grandparents taught me

My grandfather is the smartest
man I know

I have also learned a lot from my grandmother

We were spending a month in the Vermont woods writing. This was a se-
cluded spot and a small log cabin. It belonged to a friend of ours. Retired.
Now he was enjoying his well-earned rest by working harder than ever. Planting, clearing, tending his acres.

One of his grandsons had come to help him for the summer. Jim is a Har-
vard University freshman. Top student. Tennis star. The kind any grandparent would introduce with that special inflection, "This is *my* grandson."

That night we sat around the fireplace, talking. Maybe I should say, he
talked. Since he was there alone with us, he pulled out all the stops. Played
full organ on the theme: "My grandfather is the smartest man I know. I
have also learned a lot from my grandmother."

I listened with special appreciation, because he rang so many bells in me.
Here was a university student with super-sharp professors. And who was
teaching him more than all of them put together?

> My grandfather knows all the different kinds of trees. You give him a
> leaf or piece of bark and he can tell you where it came from. He can
> identify any bird's nest. We spend a lot of time in his shop and he
> teaches me how to work with tools. He has also taught me some very
> good things about plumbing and wiring. Out here you have to be able to
> repair almost anything. Then after he teaches me, he says, "You fix it,"

and most of the time I can. When I was just beginning to drive, he said, "You can go in the jeep alone now, and take care of it."

My grandmother is the same way. She has taught me how to cook and do things in the house and how to sew on a button. When she got sick last month, they didn't have to get somebody to come in, because I was there. She also knows where the wild berries grow and which mushrooms are good to eat.

My grandfather is into gardening big and I help him with planting and cultivating. I also know how to spray for bugs and set traps for animals that eat the vegetables.

Some of these things might not seem like much. But it makes life so much more interesting when you know them. It also gives you confidence.

My grandmother says, "Go ahead and cry. It will make you feel better."

My mother says it's better not to cry when my dad's around. It worries him, and then he isn't so nice to her. Whenever my brothers see me do it, they will say, "Cry baby, cry baby," so then I go to my grandparents' house. My grandmother says, "Go ahead and cry. It will make you feel better."

That man I met the other day. The one with those hard lines around his mouth. Poker face. Expression zero. What made him that rigid? Who did it? What kind of parents did he have?

Would he have done better with grandparents who encouraged him to feel his feelings?

My grandfather taught me, "There are two ways to make yourself miserable!"

The first is forever to be saying, "If only." Right on, grandpa.

> It can ruin our happiness.
> It can spoil our memories.
> It can make us a bore.

There are many versions:

"Why did we move here instead of there?"

"Why didn't we take that offer and turn down this one?"

"I should have made that phone call . . . bought that stock . . . written the letter . . . apologized."

"Couldn't we have warned them a few days sooner?"

"What would have happened 'if only'?"

"He said another way to make yourself miserable is to keep worrying, 'What if?'"

What if he has an accident?

What if the check doesn't come?

What if it's something the doctor can't cure?

What if I'm left alone?

We really can destroy our future with imagination gone berserk, and make ourselves most unattractive in the doing.

Perhaps I should take a page from this grandfather's manual. Maybe my grandchildren need this word from me.

Two certain kill-joys:
"If only"
"What if"

My grandmother is always telling me some of the things she thought were pretty awful turned out good

The right word at the right time is a skill to be learned. And when we learn it, we can bring some gifts to a grandchild for long remembering. We teach by story too and here is one passed down to me:

Once off some northern coast a storm was brewing. The fishermen were preparing to set out for one more haul. Their season was drawing to a close and they needed this run to hold them through the winter. Their wives pleaded with them not to go. But they went.

They made their haul, a big one. Then as they headed home, the sky blackened, winds blew, and the rains came. Vicious. High waves. And at last the worst. They lost their sense of direction.

In their anxiety the wives met. They met at the boathouse to pray. But suddenly up on the hill, a fire. Somebody's house was burning. So they rushed to the scene. Too late. What happened?

Annie knew what happened. She was a young bride, inexperienced, and she had left the candle burning.

As they stood helpless before the flames, they heard a shout from shore. The men! They'd made it!

With happy calls and laughter, they ran to celebrate. Except for Annie. After the first big welcome, she hung her head and sobbed, "Eric, I don't know how to tell you. I left the candle burning. Our home is gone."

What will a man do with news like that?

66

Maybe knowing what he knows, he will do what Eric did. Slipping his big fisherman's arms around his sobbing bride, he said, "Annie, you mustn't cry. It was the light from our burning cottage which brought us home."

I must remember to tell that story to my grandchildren.

Grandpa and the dead dog

What my grandfather taught me when my dog got killed:

"He sat down beside me on the back steps when I was feeling very bad. Then he said, 'Ronnie, it is all right to cry for yourself, but don't cry for Ranger. Some people wonder if there are dogs in heaven, but you know there's got to be. Heaven is where people are happy. Right? How could you be happy without a dog? So Ranger is having fun. If you only cry for you and don't cry for him, it won't be half so bad.'

"Then I did what he told me and it wasn't. I will always remember that."

Grandpa, you're pathetic. Seventy-three years, and nothing but money

He was an old man, snow-white hair, perfectly groomed, paragon of good grace, eloquent. But life had gone dead for him. He was rich, and anything money could buy, he could buy it.

Yet it all tumbled in one day when his grandson told him off. The boy had come to report:

"Thanks for the offer, but . . ."

He had decided to take the teaching job instead of that one with his grandfather's bank.

"What! Are you out of your mind? No money teaching retarded boys! You know how it is here. Good salary, benefits, promotion. I'll personally see to your promotion."

That's when his grandson let him have it:

"Grandpa, you're pathetic. Seventy-three years, and nothing but money."

That night it all caved in. Something gave way in the old man's heart. We were standing in the garden, looking at his roses, kept well by the gardener. See the pool over there, the house, the very best. Yet one thing wasn't the best. This was the way his grandson felt.

Did his other grandchildren share that feeling? His own children? His wife?

What would you say to comfort the man? He wanted money. He got it.

Of course I didn't say it, and you wouldn't. Nobody needed to say it. His grandson was saying it all with one word, "pathetic."

Children learn in reverse. Grandchildren learn in reverse.

What am I doing today, or not doing, which might come back negative?

Everybody is hurting a little
bit somewhere

Long before I was a grandfather, I met two interesting grandmothers. That's not quite true. One of them was a drag. They were charter members of my church. So I called on each of them regularly.

The lovely one was ninety-two and it was a high privilege to visit her. I always came away feeling better. Since others felt like I did, she had a host of friends. She was everybody's favorite. She simply radiated optimism. Her walls were arrayed with homey pictures. Her house was filled with flowers and plants. There was a gentle serenity as though she knew some secrets you'd like to know.

A few blocks down the street lived a woman of eighty-eight. I always went to her house first to get it over with. But now and then I lucked out: she wasn't home. That isn't even nice to say, is it? Well, she wasn't nice to call on. As a matter of fact, I'd almost rather take a clobbering than go to see her again. And that's what I'd get, clobbered.

> "Nobody ever comes to see me. Guess the church doesn't care about
> us old-timers anymore. And me a charter member. Friends, hah! Why
> even my children don't stop by like they used to."

Criticism. Censure, Gripe, gripe, gripe.

It was a repeat pattern every time I made these visits. Upbeat. Downbeat. So I began a study. What made the difference? Gradually I came to know them both well. Knew their backgrounds. They talked about their early happenings, the things which shaped them. And there was surprising little difference. Each had lived her life in that community. Each had been mar-

ried to a civic leader. Each had a long record of service in the Sunday School, women's group, committees too numerous to mention. They were regular worshipers. Could it be money? No. They both had enough to keep them comfortably. Tragedy? Did the fates come down harder over here than over there? Not really. Both had buried husband, children, brothers, sisters, friends. Operation, hospitalization? Little difference there too.

Nobody can tell for sure what makes this person walk in the sun, that person go in shadows. But I kept looking, asking. And here's what I decided:

Part of the difference was plain old habit. And the way I discovered this was something Mrs. White told me.

One day when we were philosophizing, I asked her to clue me in. How could I get what she had, be like she was? And I think the answer she gave me is one of the most profound statements I ever heard for relationships:

> "A long time ago I learned a secret. I learned that everybody is hurting a little bit somewhere. I have to keep telling myself to remember this. No matter what they ask, most folks don't really want to know about me. They want me to know about them."

That's another thing I must remember. And the older I get the more I must remember it. Plus I must remember to discuss it with my grand-children.

God doesn't expect us to do everything

Grandpa was working on the gate when a small boy appeared. He puzzled a while as small boys will. Then he asked, "Whatcha' doin', grandpa?"

To which the aged sage replied, "Sonny, there are five kinds of broken things in this old world.

"There's the kind which, when they are broken, can never be fixed.

"Then there's the kind that'll fix themselves if you leave them alone.

"There's also the kind which are none of my business. Somebody else has got to fix them.

"There's the kind which, when they are broken, you should never worry about. Them only God can fix.

"And then there's the kind I got to fix. That's what I'm doing. Fixin' this gate."

Wouldn't it be fine if my grandchildren could also learn this from me:

> God doesn't expect
> us to do everything.

Some of the world's best educators are grandparents

A few of the wisest folks I've known were short on formal education. Yet long on wisdom.

Skipper was night watchman at our seminary. I served one year as his assistant. Checking time clocks. Checking gates. Checking lovers in the bushes. And because he knew a need when he saw it, he'd sit me down on the steps and share himself with me. Or to tell it more like it was, he let me share myself with him. Chicago is a massive city for a small-town boy from Iowa. Lonesome. Especially when you've left your girl back home.

So Skipper encouraged me, guided me, taught me. Every day those seminary years I was sitting at the feet of some brilliant scholars. There were writers of erudite papers, language experts, professors of Greek and Hebrew, psychiatrists.

I passed their courses, hallelujah!

But the one from whom I learned the most was Skipper. He knew life, and love, and how to manage the inner man. How to wait.

Somebody has to be the favorite prof, and mine was Skipper. Not that I didn't like the others (most of them), but Skipper seemed to have it together. Brains, plus soul, plus how-to.

No big thing, maybe. But then again maybe it was, since Skipper had never finished junior high. At fourteen he had to check out. Somebody needs to feed the family, buy clothes, pay rent. And even when a mother is doing her best, sometimes the oldest brother has to add his best to her best.

So praise the Lord for Skipper and others like him.

Grandma Smith was like him. She was a pillar of my first little church in Colorado. Was it eleven children she had mothered? Or only ten? Thirteen? How ever many, she'd raised them well. Educated most of them. Brought them up alone. What else can you do when you're six months pregnant and they come from the railroad yard to say, "Sorry, Mrs. Smith, there's been an accident."

Where do you find the courage? The wisdom? If you're like Grandma Smith, you read the Book of Job. You go often to the writings of Paul, the Psalms, and Hebrews, chapter eleven.

Then one day you're ready for a special session with your pastor. He's young, but he's your pastor. You rock while he sits on the floor, drinks your milk, eats your cookies. You know he has problems. You know he knows what you've been through so you know what he means when he says, "How do you handle the hard things, grandma? How do I get what you've got?"

You muse a bit to his question. And then you tell him one of the wisest things he's ever heard. You tell him, "When there are troubles around me, son, I make certain they aren't inside me."

Then in the weeks to come you share your thoughts with him. You tell him what you have learned about prayer, meditation, Bible reading, loving the unlovable. You teach him about preparing ahead for problems sure to be coming. You show him how to build and fill and keep an inner reservoir.

the grief of those whom thou hast wounded.

27 Add iniquity unto their iniquity: and let them not come into thy righteousness.

28 Let them be blotted out of the book of the living, and not be written with the righteous.

29 But I *am* poor and sorrowful: let thy salvation, O God, set me up on high.

30 I will praise the name of God with a song, and will magnify him with thanksgiving.

31 *This* also shall please the LORD better than an ox *or* bullock that hath horns and hoofs.

32 The humble shall see *this, and* be glad: and your heart shall live that seek God.

33 For the LORD heareth the poor, and despiseth not his prisoners.

34 Let the heaven and earth praise him, the seas, and every thing that moveth therein.

35 For God will save Zion, and will build the cities of Judah: that they may dwell there, and have it in possession.

36 The seed also of his servants shall inherit it: and they that love his name shall dwell therein.

PSALM 70

To the chief Musician, *A Psalm of David, to bring to remembrance.*

MAKE haste, O God, *to* deliver me; make haste to help me, O LORD.

2 Let them be ashamed and confounded that seek after my soul: let them be turned backward, and put to confusion, that desire my hurt.

3 Let them be turned back for a reward of their shame that say, Aha, aha.

joice and be glad in thee: and let such as love thy salvation say continually, Let God be magnified.

5 But I *am* poor and needy: make haste unto me, O God: thou *art* my help and my deliverer; O LORD, make no tarrying.

PSALM 71

IN thee, O LORD, do I put my trust: let me never be put to confusion.

2 Deliver me in thy righteousness, and cause me to escape: incline thine ear unto me, and save me.

3 Be thou my strong habitation, whereunto I may continually resort: thou hast given commandment to save me; for thou *art* my rock and my fortress.

4 Deliver me, O my God, out of the hand of the wicked, out of the hand of the unrighteous and cruel man.

5 For thou *art* my hope, O Lord GOD: *thou art* my trust from my youth.

6 By thee have I been holden up from the womb: thou art he that took me out of my mother's bowels: my praise shall be continually of thee.

7 I am as a wonder unto many; but thou *art* my strong refuge.

8 Let my mouth be filled *with* thy praise *and with* thy honour all the day.

9 Cast me not off in the time of old age; forsake me not when my strength faileth.

10 For mine enemies speak against me; and they that lay wait for my soul take counsel together,

I have learned from books and I love to read. I have also learned from travel, and I enjoy that too. Courses, conferences, seminars, forums—these all have taught me. And I am grateful. But more than anything, anywhere, any way, I've learned from people. People like Skipper. Like Grandma Smith. Like Charlie Wall.

Charlie Wall was my packing plant foreman those two summers I spent in the rendering works. He taught me so much about toughing it out.

Then there was Axel Mandeen, builder of big buildings. Head foreman for one of the nation's major contractors. Hundreds of men worked for Axel. Thousands. And he was one of the best I've ever seen in how to handle people. How to motivate. Axel didn't go to school, like Charlie Wall didn't. And the reason they didn't was because they couldn't. Yet they taught me how to live, how to get along, how to work. From things they said, from things I saw, from things I felt when I was with them, I learned.

So I've come to this conclusion: Formal education is a good thing. I'm glad I had mine. But learning how to live and sharing that is an even better thing. This fascinates me when I wander back through my history. Many of the best educators I ever had were "uneducated."

FACT: My grandchildren are receiving some of the finest education our day has to offer. But could it be they can also learn from me?

III

What grandparents tell me to tell other grandparents

The Fun Family Forum is a bunch of fun. It's about having fun at home. About fun for moms, dads, children, teens. It's also about serious living together and things which aren't much fun.

I've been conducting these events for some years now. And lately I've added a session for grandparents. The reason for including this is something a committee chairman said: "You seem to have one blind spot. On reading your promotion some of our older folks complained, 'There is something here for everyone but us.'" And they were right. So we added a get-together for grandpas and grandmas.

They came.

They came like crazy.

They came like someone had forgotten them up to now. They came ready to talk, ready to share, ready to tell me so many things I needed to hear. Almost without exception they left me with much more than I could have given them.

So in the following section I'd like to present what grandparents tell me to tell other grandparents.

Better I keep my big mouth shut

Letter from a grandfather, hurting:

> Our grandson came to visit us this weekend and it was a terrible experience.
>
> Kevin has been a favorite of ours. Such a fine boy. He's a top-notch pitcher and an excellent student. But this year he's in college and we couldn't believe the change. He's let his hair grow long and stringy. Also it's dirty. So are his clothes and his feet and his fingernails. Plain dirty.
>
> But the worst is his attitude. We could hardly believe that either. He's questioning all the old values we know he grew up on. Says the only reason he's playing baseball is to keep his scholarship and that's not like Kevin. He's always been a great competitor.
>
> His grandmother and I discussed it and we didn't know whether to tell him how we felt. The problem is that his college isn't far away, so he'll be coming to see us often.
>
> Should we let him have it or should we hold our tongue? Do you know other grandparents who have this problem and what do they do?

Yes, I know other grandparents who have this problem. Too many. And because I do, I've read that letter at our session for grandpas and grandmas. Then I've presented this query sheet:

If you were Kevin's grandparents, would you

1. Let him have it. Give him the shock treatment. Tell him in no uncertain terms how repulsive he is. Fire away._____
2. Wait till he's gone and write him a letter.____
3. Talk to his parents and tell them how disappointed you are.____
4. Or would you say, "You can go ahead and live like that at school. But before you come here: Clean up____. Cut your hair____. Wash it____. Try to show a better attitude____."
5. Other_____.

The first time I used this little test, from back in the room a red-haired grandmother stood. "See my red hair!" she began. "I'm the kind who likes to say what I think and it hasn't been always so good. But I want you to know I've learned most of the time with my grandchildren it's better I keep my big mouth shut."

Added thought for a bit of pondering:

I must break the habit of loving my grandchild only for what he *was*. Maybe he can't become what he needs to be without someone loving him as he *is* right now.

One at a time

They have a summer home in Maine. Every year Dr. and Mrs. Eby invite their grandchildren for a visit. And they have made a new ruling:

> "When we first started this, we would invite two or three together. Sometimes all of them at once. But that was strictly no good. They fought, they pouted, they competed for attention. So we made a new rule: one at a time!
>
> "Since then it's so much better for us. We find they like it better too when we concentrate totally on one."

Input from another friend:

Things to remember when my grandchildren are coming:

1. Take it slow. They should get to know us before we smother them with love. They'll come around sooner if we let them make the first move.

2. Even if we had great rapport last time, maybe they've changed since the last visit.

3. Be wary of too many gifts. Even if I am a loving "softie," I don't want to be associated only with presents.

4. If their parents are with them, I should never interfere. If I can't take it, I should go for a walk. Maybe their parents are wrong. But counteractions from me will probably make it worse.

5. If they're here on an extended stay, I shouldn't put aside all my routines. Adjusting to my routines can be part of their education. So some of the time I'll hire a baby-sitter and go. They may even like me better if I'm not hovering every minute.

Are we doing it for them or for us?

"We built each of our three granddaughters an unusual doll house. Really a work of art if we do say so ourselves. And great fun to build. Granddaughter number one loved hers. Played with it by the hour. She called in her friends. So, spurred on by the success of doll house one, we built two more for the next granddaughters. Ho hum! They received their gifts with a respectable amount of gratitude. But the excitement wasn't there. Mild interest. Little playtime. Was it because they were second in line, and third? Or just that each is an individual?"

Good question for grandparent checking:
   Are we doing what we're doing for them or for us?

I think they like to be proud of us

From a grandmother:

"I try to keep myself up. You know what I mean? Neat and attractive so they like to come to my house. So they are proud to introduce me to their friends."

An honest Junior Higher:

"I like some things about my grandmother. But I don't like to go to her house. It is a mess. It seems like she never gets rid of anything. Like she has all these old magazines. Her closet is full of old, old dresses. There are flowerpots with nothing in them. Old pictures. Old lamp shades. Old road maps. She has a bird cage in her hallway, and she doesn't even have a bird. You can find cracked dishes and old pieces of cloth. When you open the door, it even smells like old stuff, and that is why I don't like it."

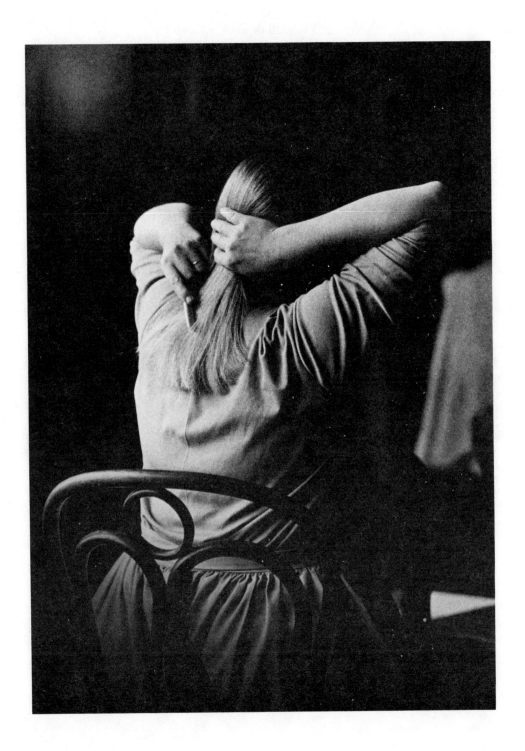

More goals:

An inviting kind of home. An appealing kind of me. And an attractive spirit, too.

> When you get to heaven
> You will doubtless view
> Many folks whose presence
>   there
> Will be a shock to you.
>
> But do not look astonished
> Do not even stare
> Doubtless there'll be
>   many folks
> Surprised to see you there.

This grandchild says:

"At our house it seems like we are always putting everybody down. Sometimes I get tired of this. When I go to my grandparents' house, my granddad says that everybody has a best side, and you will get along better if you try to see that. Some grandparents are crabby. They think the world isn't any good, and people aren't either. Mine aren't like that."

A grandpa learned:

"After we retire I think it is very important to keep in contact with people. I was getting stodgy. Then I volunteered to run the registration desk at the Boys Club. It really woke me up to kids and how they feel about things. I like to believe this will make me a better grandfather."

It could have been corns, callouses, arthritis, bursitis, rheumatism. "Oh my aching back." "Bifocals." "This blasted hearing aid."

So easy to fall into habits of groaning and moaning, "Who hath woe?"

And why shouldn't we let the world know how we are feeling?

To which there is only one answer. Nobody cares that much really. Or not many people. They want to tell us where they hurt.

One grandmother at a seminar gave us this wise word (she lives in a home for senior citizens):

> "Since I moved in here we gather on the park bench each morning. Everybody talks about his aches and pains. Only I notice nobody ever listens. We just talk. Yet I think it's got to be good for us to get it out of our system."

Sure has to be, grandma. Nothing more unattractive than a carping senior citizen. Keep it up too long and everyone tunes us out, including our grandchildren.

One "oh-won't-you-feel-sorry-for-me" gal got it done by epitaph. Not a bad idea, maybe. At least she provided a laugh when she made a deal with her monument maker and he carved on her stone:

SEE, I TOLD YOU I WAS SICK

Thoughts on baby-sitting

"Do I love my grandchildren! Almost any time I'd give five dollars to see them come. Two weeks later (should I even tell you this?), I'd give ten dollars to see them go."

"If you live close, you better have a clear understanding that you will baby-sit when *you* want to. Of course, we should make exceptions in emergencies. But I have this friend whose children really *use* her, and it's degrading."

"I think we should see our grandchildren because we love them. I even think we should talk this over with their parents. They can get them ready for coming to our house. What I mean is, they get them ready for a lot of love and fun. In other words, don't just drop them off on us."

"That makes sense. But when it's time for them to go home, we should get them ready for that too."

"One way to get control is to offer your services when you feel like it. It must be embarrassing if they always have to ask, 'Will you baby-sit?'"

"I'm a salesman. I travel some every week. During the summer I take each of my grandchildren along for a trip or two. This is absolutely the greatest. We have more fun. Besides, I think they're learning quite a bit about people and selling and business. This year we decided the oldest one is ready to go on a vacation with us. Three weeks. That'll be something, won't it?"

I think it's important we make them behave

Grandma One:

My mother used a yardstick on me and I don't hesitate to give it to my grandchildren when they've got it coming. If they're at my house, they're going to do things my way.

Two:

I think it's important for us to know what kind of discipline they're accustomed to. It seems to me consistency between parents and grandparents would be wise.

Three:

Only discipline when you're in charge. When the parents are around, let them handle it.

Four:

I could never lay a hand on one of my grandchildren except in love. They know I won't. But I can honestly tell you they aren't all that bad when they're with us. I wonder if it's because they aren't afraid.

If you fuss too much, they'll do it again

We had been discussing some of the sticky little problems at this session. We'd talked about the small fibs and outright lies.

There were numerous good ideas from many sources, but none better than this from Jessie May. Some of us knew Jessie May, and we knew she knew a thing or two. Seven children. Eleven grandchildren. Plus she'd been part-time mother to a miscellaneous assortment of others.

Jessie May:

> I've found the less you fuss over things they're going to outgrow anyway, the better. If you fuss too much, you watch. They'll do it again just for excitement.

No way!

Two excellent words for our grandparenting, "No way." "No" may have been good enough in days gone by. Today it seems to imply there is an opening around here somewhere. These days "No way" is the final word. "Every door is closed, Junior!" "That's it!" "No way!"

Don't lower your standards because they do

Letter from grandparents:

"We attended one of your seminars, but we have a problem we were embarrassed to bring up.

"Our granddaughter is coming to see us for her spring holidays. And under normal circumstances we would be looking forward to her visit. Only this time she has written us what she calls an honest letter, telling us something that breaks our hearts. She has been living in an apartment with some man. She's going into a long explanation that you've probably heard before. But the thing which bothers us is that she's asking if she can bring him with her and can they stay together at our house.

"Should we say, 'You're welcome, but he isn't.' Or 'You can bring him along, but he can't stay here.'

"If we tell her what we believe, won't she think we're old-fashioned?

"We're so confused. Can you help us?"

Wish I could. This kind of thing comes often these days.

So what can we do?

One thing we can do is stand our ground. I find this often in the young set —even if they disagree, they want to know, does anyone believe anything anymore?

Condemning, scolding, preaching are not the answer. But plain old-fashioned ethics from grandparents, they'll buy these if we say it right.

And how can we say it right?

Here's one grandfather's answer: "I'd tell her, 'You can sleep in the bedroom and he can sleep on the couch.'"

That's not all the man said. He also added, "I'll be up in the night to check you out."

Would you say that? Would I?

Yes, the first part! But I'd leave off at that "Check you out" line. These are grown people. I would extend them the dignity of deciding for themselves. Would they accept the invitation on our terms? And if they did, I'd expect them to live our way at our house.

Is it so bad to have favorites?

Most of us never outgrow the tendency to guilty feelings. Grandpas and grandmas are no exception. In our grandparenting seminars some tricky old problems push over tombstones where we thought we had buried them. Maybe it's no big thing. But then again what do we do when it's a fact:

We like one grandchild better than the others?

One thing we do is to remember our Creator put us together this way. We are naturally drawn to some people. Others aren't so attractive. Then there are those we can hardly take.

That's true of the general populace, the neighbors, kinfolk of every kind.

Even grandchildren.

Even if it takes longer

Young father:

"I wish I could have a little carpenter shop, make things, fix things. But I've never been any good with my hands. You know what I think? I think it's my dad's fault. He would take me out to his shop and show me how he built things. But then he would give me holy hell if I didn't do it like he wanted it.

"Do you think that could be why tools make me nervous?"

Yes, I think it could be.

A grandfather:

"One of the best things we ever did was to give the kids a little room at our house where they could make any kind of mess they wanted. It wasn't really a room, actually only a closet. But they sure loved it."

A grandchild:

"Grandparents let you do things all by yourself even if it takes longer and doesn't look too good."

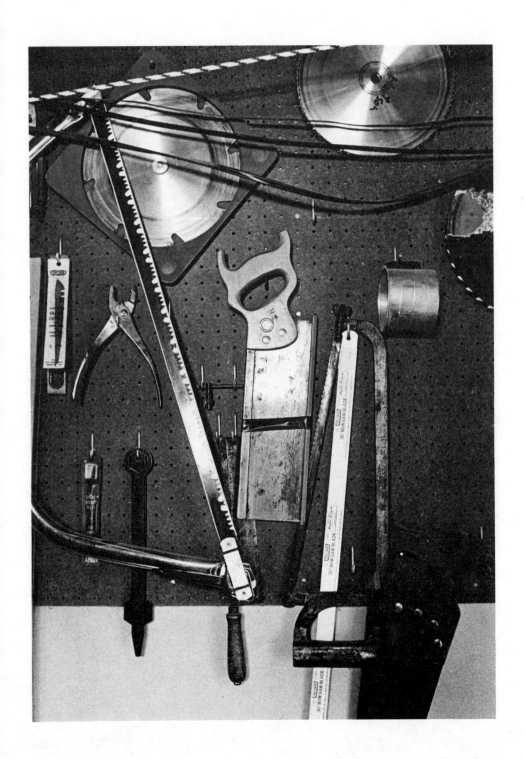

All children need certain places which will always be the same

A child psychologist friend of mine says:

> *All children need certain places which will always be the same. This gives them security.*

The McCormicks live in California. They're retired now, doing their thing in many interesting ways. They're especially strong on church work, real servants of the Lord. They fit in so many places where quiet people make a big difference.

The McCormicks are also fun grandparents, and here's one thing they did. As each grandchild reached a certain age, grandpa McCormick built a little wooden box for that particular child. Barbara Ann, Stephen, Todd, Melanie, Gretchen. Then when they came to visit, grandma said, "You go up to the attic, take anything you find there you'd like to have for your own. Put it in your box and it will be yours forever."

Barbara Ann is married now. She has two children of her own. That makes the McCormicks great-grandparents and it also makes them somebody special to visit.

Barbara Ann brings her family three or four times each year. And here are the lines I like: "You'd think an adult might outgrow some things, wouldn't you? But it's a fact. Barbara Ann isn't in the house very long until she makes a trip to the attic just to be with her box."

In our mobile generation, this could be a real winner for good grandparenting.

Those side doors are important

Lots of beautiful people in Ohio, including Mrs. Allen. Nine times a grandmother.

Astute word from Mrs. Allen:

> "My grandchildren have always lived somewhere near me. So I regularly would let each of them come and spend a weekend. We'd always do what they wanted to do. I can't think of many things I haven't been to. Rock concerts, ball games, shows I'd never go to on my own. The zoo. A float trip down the river."

What's so unusual about all this? Lots of grandparents have done as much. But here comes the smart part.

Mrs. Allen adds:

> "As soon as they get to be teenagers, I make excuses so they won't have to do things with me any more. I think those side doors are important when they get to their teens. They still come see me. They come for an evening or a weekend, but it's because *they* want to. And sometimes when they're in college, or even after they're married, they'll say, 'Grandma, remember how we used to go out together? Let's do it again. I need a visit.'"

Epilogue: *Love, and the Lord, and heaven too*

Grandparents are for holding hands and smiling at each other

It was late. The basketball game was over and we had adjourned to a restaurant. I had come to speak at a small college. The committee had met me at the plane and driven me to the game. We won, so everyone was feeling super. Now we were getting acquainted, talking plans.

Not much of a restaurant. Towns like this roll up their better places early, so everybody comes here. "Everybody" that night included the ballplayers, students, faculty. Plus ex-faculty.

In the booth across from us, a small drama unfolded. Simple vignette, but oh, the meaning. They were an elderly couple, very elderly, like eighty-plus. After they made their rounds of greeting, they chose their spot. And I'm glad they sat where they did. It was in direct line with my vision. I could hardly keep my eyes off them. That was all right. They only had eyes for each other.

Smiling. Whispering. Laughing. Plus every now and then he would pat her hand. Then she would look at him like something out of a storybook.

I wasn't the only one who saw it. One of the guys in our booth, observing me observing them, mused, "How about those two? Aren't they something?" Another explained this was the ex-college president. He'd been here forever. Emeritus now. Big basketball fan. Actually fan of everything on campus. His wife liked it all too. But mostly they were obvious fans of each other.

Into the conversation came now a question, the kind with variant meanings: "Aren't they silly?"

"Yeah," said one of the girls from deep in her soul. "And I should be so lucky."

Then she went on to say that just this week she and her girl friends had been talking about the lovers. For three years she'd been watching them herself. And most of her friends, she said, would join in her wish. Wouldn't it be wonderful if when they were eighty-plus they would have a love like that?

The young set will rap forever on "How can I know I'm really in love?" "How can I be sure we will be happy together?" "How involved can we be without hurting each other?"

Necking, petting, sex, living together, not living together, what's safe, what isn't. These all are favorite themes. Run them by again. Play the record over.

Yet meaningful as these things are, there is one thing even more meaningful than discussing love.

That's seeing it.

And the Lord has equipped the wisest of the young set with a kind of radar vision. It looks right through the unreal to know the authentic.

Premarriage counseling is big these days. Many churches require it. Most schools offer some guidance in how to get along close up. Everyone of these, fine. But my wife and I have learned another thing from working with them. Studying love from a book . . . hearing about it in consultation . . . speakers . . . seminars . . . retreats . . . these are not the most effective media.

Number one is demonstration. To see a beautiful relationship has to be the ultimate.

> "Lord, help us to be exhibit 'A' of
> a good thing going in married love."

You're right. We should say exhibit "B." Everyone of us would pray that exhibit "A" might be their mother and dad. But whether that's true or isn't, we do have this additional plus—more years of loving.

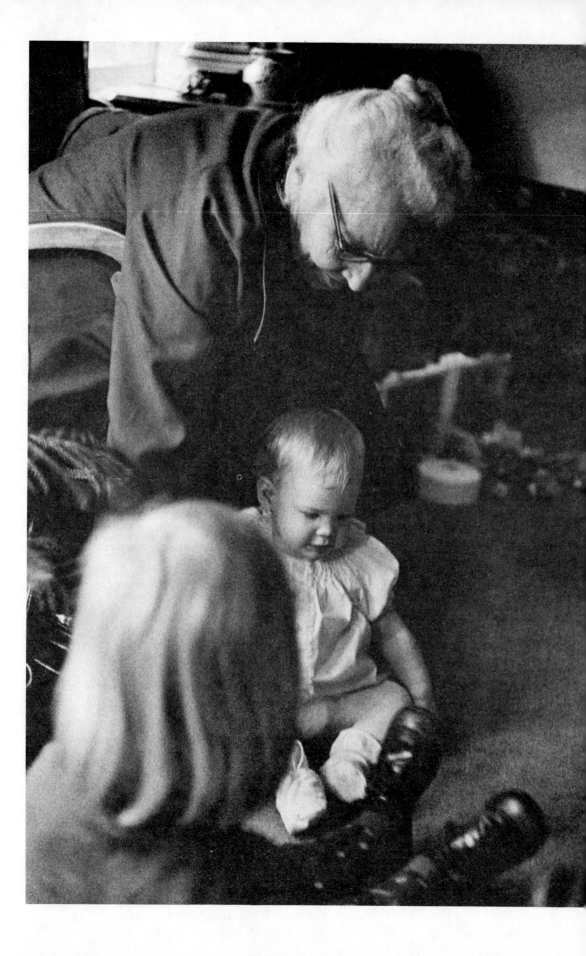

I have known well more than a dozen old couples who reached their fiftieth anniversary. And three who went as far as sixty years of togetherness. They represent a wide range of income, status, influence. Some of these men I've known very well. The weather-beaten farmer in Nebraska. The smooth-faced metropolitan banker. Schoolhouse janitor in crossroad town. President of a major publishing firm. They all had one thing in common. They learned to share themselves in total companionship.

That's a great word, "companionship." It takes on added significance as the years pass. Physical needs might fade, and excitement diminish too. Money worries subside. Responsibilities go. But there is one thing wise lovers keep constantly on the increase. This is the gradual opening of two hearts to welcome each other at the core of their beings.

And those who accomplish it may be doing much more than something for themselves alone. Who knows where this witness goes? When will it strengthen someone? Give hope? Meaning?

Maybe the very best happenings from loving each other well are seen from the eyes of our grandchildren. The little girl said a big thing, didn't she?

"Grandparents are for
holding hands and
smiling at each other."

My grandmother makes me think that God is her best friend

The phone rang. Police. Could I come right away? This was a small town where they depended on the ministers. So I went. And when I arrived, something I'd never seen before.

An attractive young woman was sitting on a chair, asking, "Who am I?"

She rose, paced the floor, sat down again. She shook her head, rapped at her forehead, and asked it over and over, "Who am I? Who am I?"

Turned out she was a jewelry salesgirl for the sorority circuits. But nobody knew that until some time later. Finally, after a few days' rest in the hospital, and some excellent detective work, she began to get it together. She remembered who she was.

They call it amnesia. She'd been in an accident. Someone brought her in and left her at the station. Why had they failed to identify themselves? Were they afraid they might be blamed for her damaged car? But however many questions unanswered, this one thing was for sure: We would never forget the scene, as she put her face to the face of people she didn't know. Anxious. Puzzled. Querying, "Who am I?"

It's the parable of every man, every woman. This thing inside me needs to know, "Am I more than an accident along the highway? Does life have meaning I've missed? Anybody know?"

No problem to get the young set rapping on religion. If we come at it right, this can be one of the most popular subjects in colleges and high schools. They'll tie right into it, discuss, philosophize. And much of the time, like the soothsayer said, come out the same door by which they went in.

Seminaries, graduate schools, Bible colleges, summer camps, weekend re-treats—they've done their good. A lot of it maybe.

Yet when it comes to theology in its purest form, can anything surpass this?

> "My grandmother makes me think
> that God is her best friend."

And then she added this profound word (I thought it profound for a high school senior):

> "I hope I can know Him that way too."

Wouldn't that be wonderful for all of us?

And especially for our grandchildren.

Sometimes when it is quiet, they will even talk to you about heaven

The small boy said it and I was surprised. But I shouldn't have been. Today's young minds, even the youngest, simply won't settle for zero.

Grade school, junior high, high school, and especially in college they're saying, "See what I found in the wastebasket.

"Could it be true?

"Is it possible?

"Does life really go on?

"Wouldn't it be fun if this forever and forever stuff was for me and my friends?"

And who is wise enough to handle these themes enormous? Someone who has had plenty of time to think? Like a grandparent? Will they most likely be heard?

To which there is only one answer. They will. Love and the Lord, and heaven too can have the feel of the real when they come from a grandmother, grandfather.

Timothy was thirteen when his grandmother died. Same one you could ask, "Why isn't milk green?" It's devastating for a boy to lose his best friend at thirteen. Plus it's like a tree going down outside the window for the rest of us.

Cards from many places, letters, phone calls, telegrams. Comforters coming by the dozen. She had so many friends. But the thing which supported us most, all of our family, was this unabashed word from our seventh-grader:

Do you know what I like to think about now? It is how grandma and I would sit and talk about heaven. She talked mostly about seeing grandpa again. And her baby girl. Then we would discuss it. Would she still be a baby or grown now? And do you know what we decided? We decided heaven is how you want it.

Useless wondering? Maybe! Maybe not! Maybe it's one of the best reasons for being a grandpa or grandma.

> "Sometimes when it is quiet,
> they will even talk to
> you about heaven."